Table of Cont

This lesson plan book belongs to:

Name Alice

School home

Grade/Subject ______

Room 1

School Year ______

Address ______

Phone ______

Teacher Created Resources, Inc.
12621 Western Avenue
Garden Grove, CA 92841
www.teachercreated.com
ISBN: 978-0-7439-3250-9

Reprinted, 2016
Made in U.S.A.

Managing Editor: Karen Goldfluss, M.S.Ed.
Art Director: CJae Froshay
Art Manager: Kevin Barnes
Cover Art: ©Susan Winget
Cover Design: Barb Lorseyedi
Imaging: James Edward Grace
Interior Art: ©Susan Winget

Ways to Use This Book

Seating Chart (Page 3)

A seating chart is provided for easy reference. Table or desk arrangement will vary throughout the year depending on room size, available furniture, grade level taught, teaching style, and academic program needs. To accommodate a variety of classroom arrangements, you may wish to create additional charts and place specific seating information in a separate folder.

Student Roster (Pages 4 and 5)

Record both student and parent or guardian names and addresses. Make a special note of differences in last names when appropriate. You may wish to list siblings and their grades. Notes may include children with special needs or medications that are necessary.

Birthdays (Page 6)

Use the chart on this page to write students' names and birth dates. Recognize each special day with a birthday greeting. For younger children, you may wish to sing to them.

Weekly Schedule (Page 7)

If your schedule changes periodically, you may wish to duplicate this page before completing your current schedule. Attach new schedules throughout the year, as need arises.

Year At A Glance (Pages 8 and 9)

Use this chart to plan units of study and/or focus on immediate and upcoming events, conferences, meetings, seminars, and other important dates. Record each event as soon as you are notified. The Year At A Glance chart can also be reproduced for students to help them plan projects and keep track of important dates and events.

Substitute Teacher Information (Pages 10 and 11)

Record all pertinent information on these pages. If you have a copy of the layout of your school, attach it to this page; otherwise, sketch an outline of the school grounds, showing restrooms, office, lounge, playground, etc. Attach a paper clip to both this page and the lesson page for easy reference.

Student of the Week (Pages 12 and 13)

Acknowledge the special talents and accomplishments, or reward good behavior, by recognizing students throughout the year. Use these pages to keep track of each Student of the Week.

Classroom Ideas (Page 14)

Start off the school year with these tips. Included are several ways to incorporate each idea throughout the year.

Good Writing Tips and Traits (Pages 15 and 16)

These pages provide you with information about the primary traits of good writing as well as tips for a successful writing program in your classroom.

Class Records (Pages 17–76)

The class records section is designed to provide organized space for recording daily notations or grades for assignments, tests, attendance, tardies, participation, etc. Each page contains a five-week block of spaces so that a student's record for an entire quarter of 10 weeks can be read on facing pages. A summary column for recording total attendance, tardies, and grades appear on the right-hand facing page for each ten-week period. Enough record sheets are provided to last for two 20-week semesters, accommodating seven different classes or preparations. Two extra pages of record sheets covering 10 weeks (or one quarter) are provided for copy or replacement purposes.

Lesson Plans (Pages 77–160)

Use the lesson plans to help you organize yourself each week. There are enough weekly plan pages to cover a 40-week school year. At the top of the left-hand page, fill in the blank to indicate the week dates for which the plans are written. The first column may be used for notes or reminders. Also, read the quotes and words of wisdom on the right-hand pages to inspire you throughout the week!

Seating Chart

Seat Arrangement Ideas

Sticky notes can be used to temporarily assign seats.

1. ***Basic Row Seating***

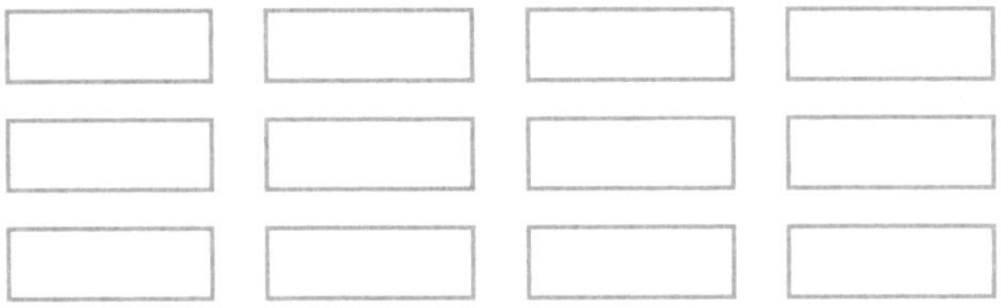

2. ***U-Shaped Seating***

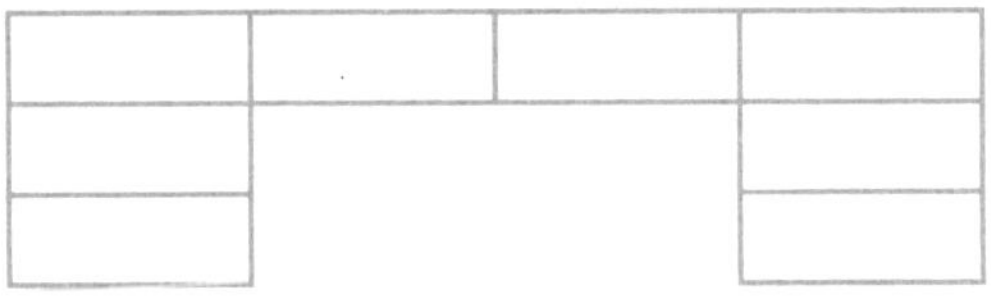

3. ***Rectangle***

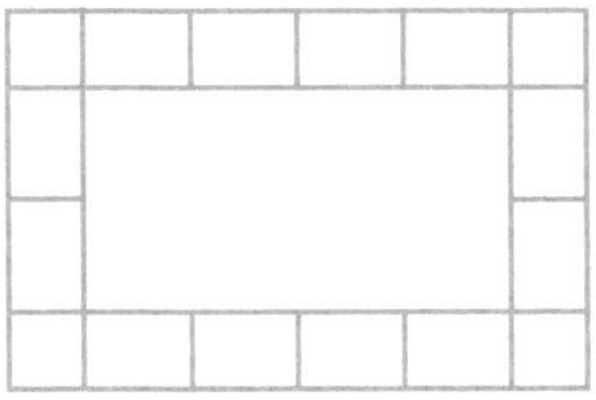

4. ***Partner Seating***

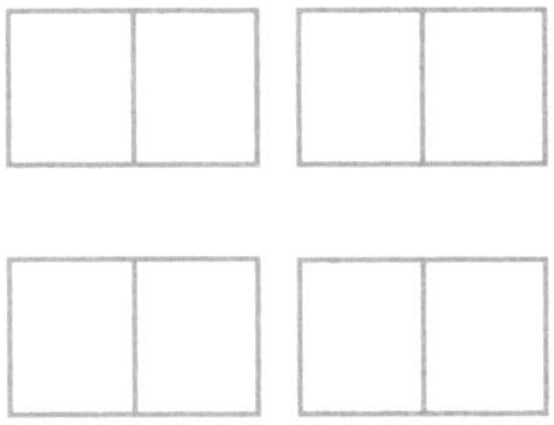

The size and shape of your room will play a large part in your seating arrangement.

You may want to change this layout once you are familiar with your students and their needs.

Regardless of your seating plan, the most important concern is that you can easily see all your students and the children in turn have good visibility of you, the chalkboard, and other focal points in the room.

Front of Classroom

Student

Student	Parent/Guardian	Address
1.		
2.		
3.		
4.		
5.		
6.		
7.		
8.		
9.		
10.		
11.		
12.		
13.		
14.		
15.		
16.		
17.		
18.		
19.		
20.		
21.		
22.		
23.		
24.		
25.		
26.		
27.		
28.		
29.		
30.		
31.		
32.		
33.		
34.		
35.		
36.		

Roster

Home & Work Phones	Birthday	Siblings	Notes

Birthdays

August	September	October
November	**December**	**January**
February	**March**	**April**
May	**June**	**July**
		aeice: 22

Weekly Schedule

Time	Monday	Tuesday	Wednesday	Thursday	Friday

Year At

<table>
<tr><th>September</th><th>October</th></tr>
<tr><td>
</td><td></td></tr>
<tr><th>January</th><th>February</th></tr>
<tr><td> </td><td>
</td></tr>
<tr><th>May</th><th>June</th></tr>
<tr><td></td><td>
</td></tr>
</table>

A Glance

November	December

March	April

July	August

Substitute Teacher Information

School Schedule

- Class Begins ____________________
- Morning Recess ____________________
- Lunchtime ____________________
- Class Resumes ____________________
- Afternoon Recess ____________________
- Dismissal ____________________

Special Notes

____
____
____
____
____
____
____
____

Special Classes

Student ____________________

Class ____________ Day ________ Time ________

Student ____________________

Class ____________ Day ________ Time ________

Student ____________________

Class ____________ Day ________ Time ________

Where to Find

- Class List ____________________
- School Layout ____________________
- Seating Chart ____________________
- Attendance Record ____________________
- Lesson Plans ____________________
- Teacher Manuals ____________________
- First Aid Kit ____________________
- Emergency Information ____________________
- Supplementary Activities ____________________
- Class Supplies–paper, pencils, etc. ____________________
- Referral Forms and Procedures ____________________

____
____
____
____
____
____
____
____
____
____
____

Special Needs Students

Student	Needs	Time and Place

Substitute Teacher Information

Classroom Standards

- When finished with an assignment
- When and how to speak out in class
- Incentive Program
- Discipline
- Restroom Procedure

People Who Can Help

- Teacher/Room ____________________
- Dependable Students ____________________
- Principal ____________________
- Secretary ____________________
- Custodian ____________________
- Counselor ____________________
- Nurse ____________________

Layout of School—including school office, faculty lounge, restrooms, auditorium, playground, etc. (or attach printed diagram here)

Student of the Week

Week of: ______________________________
Student: ______________________________

____

Week of: ______________________________
Student: ______________________________

____

Week of: ______________________________
Student: ______________________________

____

Week of: ______________________________
Student: ______________________________

____

Week of: ______________________________
Student: ______________________________

____

Week of: ______________________________
Student: ______________________________

____

Week of: ______________________________
Student: ______________________________

____

Week of: ______________________________
Student: ______________________________

____

Week of: ______________________________
Student: ______________________________

____

Week of: ______________________________
Student: ______________________________

____

Week of: ______________________________
Student: ______________________________

____

Week of: ______________________________
Student: ______________________________

____

Week of: ______________________________
Student: ______________________________

____

Week of: ______________________________
Student: ______________________________

____

Week of: ______________________________
Student: ______________________________

____

Week of: ______________________________
Student: ______________________________

____

Week of: ______________________________
Student: ______________________________

____

Week of: ______________________________
Student: ______________________________

____

Week of: ______________________________
Student: ______________________________

____

Week of: ______________________________
Student: ______________________________

____

Student of the Week

Week of: ____________________
Student: ____________________

Week of: ____________________
Student: ____________________

Week of: ____________________
Student: ____________________

Week of: ____________________
Student: ____________________

Week of: ____________________
Student: ____________________

Week of: ____________________
Student: ____________________

Week of: ____________________
Student: ____________________

Week of: ____________________
Student: ____________________

Week of: ____________________
Student: ____________________

Week of: ____________________
Student: ____________________

Week of: ____________________
Student: ____________________

Week of: ____________________
Student: ____________________

Week of: ____________________
Student: ____________________

Week of: ____________________
Student: ____________________

Week of: ____________________
Student: ____________________

Week of: ____________________
Student: ____________________

Week of: ____________________
Student: ____________________

Week of: ____________________
Student: ____________________

Week of: ____________________
Student: ____________________

Week of: ____________________
Student: ____________________

Classroom Ideas

Begin the year with these "Sticks, Numbers, and Bins" ideas. You will find yourself using or adapting these suggestions throughout the year.

Sticks

The sticks are large, craft sticks (tongue depressors). On the stick, place the student's name in black permanent marker. On the first day of school, give each student one stick. The student's job is to decorate it anyway he or she wishes—color both sides or one side, use markers or crayons, etc. Once complete, the stick is held in a specially designated cup where it remains all year. These sticks are used for a variety of tasks. Whenever you need a volunteer, pick a stick. To raffle off an extra item or poster, pick a stick. To get a quick partner, pick a stick. To choose a special helper for a special task, pick a stick.

Student Numbers

The numbers are given to the students for organizational purposes. However, they come in handy for other circumstances, too. In most grade books, the students' names are in alphabetical order. Next to each name is a number 1–30. Obviously, the first student in alphabetical order will be number one, and so on. At the start of the year, put the numbers on the corner of each desk using black self-adhesive numbers found at any office supply store. Those same numbers are placed on the student's homework bin, any class textbook, and on any other student material to be used throughout the year.

Why are numbers helpful? It really keeps the anonymity of the student and allows you to reuse items from year to year because there are no names on books, math manipulatives, and other classroom items. Papers and projects turned in using number order are already alphabetized for your grade book, and the teacher can use the numbers for other random events, such as having all the odd numbers line up or all the two-digit numbers get the mail.

During the first week of school, tell the students they each have a number and that it is their number all year long for everything. For example, a student named Kate Calm would be number four. Her desk will have a four on it and so will her homework bin, math tool kit, social studies book, science book, and reading novels. Any item labeled with a four would belong to Kate Calm.

Homework Bins

Homework bins are another organizational tool. Each bin is marked with a student number. This allows repeated use from year to year. Each morning the students turn in the night's homework in their bins. This works well because the teacher can collect the work in alphabetical order for grading and recording purposes. If there is no name on a paper, the papers are alphabetical so the teacher can easily find the owner. The homework bins also make it very easy to see who has not turned in his or her homework because the bin will be empty. The teacher can talk to that student immediately. It might be that he or she just forgot to turn in the homework. Now, the teacher will no longer have a pile of random papers and can quickly tell whose work is missing.

✓ **Tip:** Have a teacher mailbox on the desk for students to turn in any permission slips, notes from parents, or other forms. Keep the homework bins for student work only.

Good Writing Tips and Traits

What writing traits do you look for when you read your students' work? Current educational theory delineates several primary traits that comprise good writing. When checking and revising their work, students should be aware of these traits and whether or not their writing reflects the traits effectively. Share these writing traits with the class and encourage students to apply them throughout the year.

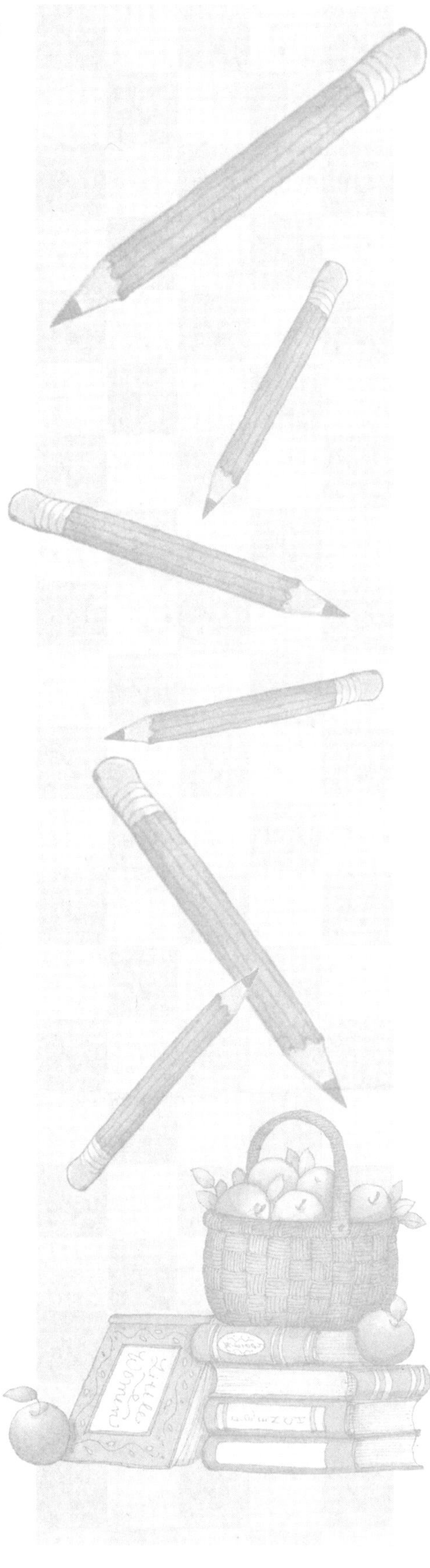

Voice

Voice is a unique quality of the writer. The writer's voice shows his or her personality. Voice sometimes sets the tone or mood of the writing.

Word Choice

Precise and careful word choice is essential for good writing. A dictionary and thesaurus should always be kept nearby when writing. However, here is a word of caution regarding the thesaurus: Students should be careful never to choose a word that is out of place with the rest of the writing.

Organization

The writing's organization is its structure. Sometimes the structure has a precise format as in a problem/solution essay, and sometimes the structure is unprecedented. In either case, the organization should be clear and easy to follow.

Conventions

Conventions are all those elements of grammar and mechanics that make writing understandable. Editing is the process completed while checking one's conventions.

Sentence Fluency

Good writers are careful to vary sentence length, to use understandable syntaxes, and to be sure that one sentence flows easily into the next. These characteristics together comprise sentence fluency.

Ideas

Ideas are the foundation of good writing. To write effectively, one's ideas must be sound, clear, and thoroughly supported.

Presentation

To emphasize their most important ideas, good writers often incorporate visual materials into their writing. This adds interest and clarity to the overall work.

Good Writing Tips and Traits

Tips for a Successful Writing Program

- Include a daily writing period in your schedule. Set aside a writing center for conferencing and storing writing folders and related materials.
- Writing time does not have to be silent time. Allow the students to collaborate. A small group, such as a writing circle, often works well.
- Conferencing is essential. During writing time, meet with a writing circle. Focus on one student's work at a time, allowing the others to observe and to offer input as well. This process should be modeled and practiced with groups to ensure a positive learning environment and comfort level for students. Let the author "run" the conference by talking through his or her own work. Teacher comments or questions should guide, not direct, the discussion.
- Keep all work in a writing folder. Students can also keep running lists of words and topics in their individual folders.
- Use student portfolios to keep all final pieces that will be or have been evaluated. Portfolios show the students' best work.
- Model and participate in all writing yourself. Let the students see the process in action. The overhead projector is an excellent modeling tool.
- Use computers, if possible. They lend a professional quality to the writing and take the drudgery out of revision.
- Illustrations or graphic representations should be encouraged.
- Display and publish writing samples contributed by a variety of students. Store some writing in class books and keep the books in your classroom library.
- Share as much student writing as possible. Students need to write for an audience as well as to hear other authors' voices. However, do not push an unwilling student into sharing.
- Never underestimate the power of a journal! Journal writing should be a daily event. Why not begin each day with a journal topic on the board and five minutes of freewrite time (with optional sharing afterwards)?

Class Records

Subject ______________________________

Week	Week ___					Week ___					Week ___					Week ___					Week ___				
Day	M	T	W	T	F	M	T	W	T	F	M	T	W	T	F	M	T	W	T	F	M	T	W	T	F
Date																									
Assignments or Attendance																									
Name																									
1																									
2																									
3																									
4																									
5																									
6																									
7																									
8																									
9																									
10																									
11																									
12																									
13																									
14																									
15																									
16																									
17																									
18																									
19																									
20																									
21																									
22																									
23																									
24																									
25																									
26																									
27																									
28																									
29																									
30																									
31																									
32																									
33																									
34																									
35																									
36																									

Period ____________________

Week____					Week____					Week____					Week____					Week____						Days Present	Days Absent	Tardies	Quarter Grade		
M	T	W	T	F	M	T	W	T	F	M	T	W	T	F	M	T	W	T	F	M	T	W	T	F							
																									1						
																									2						
																									3						
																									4						
																									5						
																									6						
																									7						
																									8						
																									9						
																									10						
																									11						
																									12						
																									13						
																									14						
																									15						
																									16						
																									17						
																									18						
																									19						
																									20						
																									21						
																									22						
																									23						
																									24						
																									25						
																									26						
																									27						
																									28						
																									29						
																									30						
																									31						
																									32						
																									33						
																									34						
																									35						
																									36						

Subject ____________________

Week	Week____					Week____					Week____					Week____					Week____				
Day	M	T	W	T	F	M	T	W	T	F	M	T	W	T	F	M	T	W	T	F	M	T	W	T	F
Date																									
Assignments or Attendance																									
Name																									
1																									
2																									
3																									
4																									
5																									
6																									
7																									
8																									
9																									
10																									
11																									
12																									
13																									
14																									
15																									
16																									
17																									
18																									
19																									
20																									
21																									
22																									
23																									
24																									
25																									
26																									
27																									
28																									
29																									
30																									
31																									
32																									
33																									
34																									
35																									
36																									

Period ________________________________

Week ____					Week ____					Week ____					Week ____					Week ____						Days Present	Days Absent	Tardies	Quarter Grade		
M	T	W	T	F	M	T	W	T	F	M	T	W	T	F	M	T	W	T	F	M	T	W	T	F							
																									1						
																									2						
																									3						
																									4						
																									5						
																									6						
																									7						
																									8						
																									9						
																									10						
																									11						
																									12						
																									13						
																									14						
																									15						
																									16						
																									17						
																									18						
																									19						
																									20						
																									21						
																									22						
																									23						
																									24						
																									25						
																									26						
																									27						
																									28						
																									29						
																									30						
																									31						
																									32						
																									33						
																									34						
																									35						
																									36						

Subject ____________________

Week	Week ____					Week ____					Week ____					Week ____					Week ____				
Day	M	T	W	T	F	M	T	W	T	F	M	T	W	T	F	M	T	W	T	F	M	T	W	T	F
Date																									
Assignments or Attendance																									
Name																									
1																									
2																									
3																									
4																									
5																									
6																									
7																									
8																									
9																									
10																									
11																									
12																									
13																									
14																									
15																									
16																									
17																									
18																									
19																									
20																									
21																									
22																									
23																									
24																									
25																									
26																									
27																									
28																									
29																									
30																									
31																									
32																									
33																									
34																									
35																									
36																									

Period ___________________________

Week ____					Week ____					Week ____					Week ____					Week ____						Days Present	Days Absent	Tardies	Quarter Grade		
M	T	W	T	F	M	T	W	T	F	M	T	W	T	F	M	T	W	T	F	M	T	W	T	F							
																									1						
																									2						
																									3						
																									4						
																									5						
																									6						
																									7						
																									8						
																									9						
																									10						
																									11						
																									12						
																									13						
																									14						
																									15						
																									16						
																									17						
																									18						
																									19						
																									20						
																									21						
																									22						
																									23						
																									24						
																									25						
																									26						
																									27						
																									28						
																									29						
																									30						
																									31						
																									32						
																									33						
																									34						
																									35						
																									36						

Subject ____________________

Week	Week____					Week____					Week____					Week____					Week____				
Day	M	T	W	T	F	M	T	W	T	F	M	T	W	T	F	M	T	W	T	F	M	T	W	T	F
Date																									
Assignments or Attendance																									
Name																									
1																									
2																									
3																									
4																									
5																									
6																									
7																									
8																									
9																									
10																									
11																									
12																									
13																									
14																									
15																									
16																									
17																									
18																									
19																									
20																									
21																									
22																									
23																									
24																									
25																									
26																									
27																									
28																									
29																									
30																									
31																									
32																									
33																									
34																									
35																									
36																									

Period ______________________________

Week____					Week____					Week____					Week____					Week____						Days Present	Days Absent	Tardies	Quarter Grade		
M	T	W	T	F	M	T	W	T	F	M	T	W	T	F	M	T	W	T	F	M	T	W	T	F							
																									1						
																									2						
																									3						
																									4						
																									5						
																									6						
																									7						
																									8						
																									9						
																									10						
																									11						
																									12						
																									13						
																									14						
																									15						
																									16						
																									17						
																									18						
																									19						
																									20						
																									21						
																									22						
																									23						
																									24						
																									25						
																									26						
																									27						
																									28						
																									29						
																									30						
																									31						
																									32						
																									33						
																									34						
																									35						
																									36						

Subject ____________________

Week	Week____					Week____					Week____					Week____					Week____				
Day	M	T	W	T	F	M	T	W	T	F	M	T	W	T	F	M	T	W	T	F	M	T	W	T	F
Date																									
Assignments or Attendance																									
Name																									
1																									
2																									
3																									
4																									
5																									
6																									
7																									
8																									
9																									
10																									
11																									
12																									
13																									
14																									
15																									
16																									
17																									
18																									
19																									
20																									
21																									
22																									
23																									
24																									
25																									
26																									
27																									
28																									
29																									
30																									
31																									
32																									
33																									
34																									
35																									
36																									

Period ____________________

Week ____					Week ____					Week ____					Week ____					Week ____						Days Present	Days Absent	Tardies	Quarter Grade		
M	T	W	T	F	M	T	W	T	F	M	T	W	T	F	M	T	W	T	F	M	T	W	T	F							
																									1						
																									2						
																									3						
																									4						
																									5						
																									6						
																									7						
																									8						
																									9						
																									10						
																									11						
																									12						
																									13						
																									14						
																									15						
																									16						
																									17						
																									18						
																									19						
																									20						
																									21						
																									22						
																									23						
																									24						
																									25						
																									26						
																									27						
																									28						
																									29						
																									30						
																									31						
																									32						
																									33						
																									34						
																									35						
																									36						

Subject ____________________

Week	Week____					Week____					Week____					Week____					Week____				
Day	M	T	W	T	F	M	T	W	T	F	M	T	W	T	F	M	T	W	T	F	M	T	W	T	F
Date																									
Assignments or Attendance																									
Name																									
1																									
2																									
3																									
4																									
5																									
6																									
7																									
8																									
9																									
10																									
11																									
12																									
13																									
14																									
15																									
16																									
17																									
18																									
19																									
20																									
21																									
22																									
23																									
24																									
25																									
26																									
27																									
28																									
29																									
30																									
31																									
32																									
33																									
34																									
35																									
36																									

Period ________________

Week____					Week____					Week____					Week____					Week____						*Days Present*	*Days Absent*	*Tardies*	*Quarter Grade*		
M	T	W	T	F	M	T	W	T	F	M	T	W	T	F	M	T	W	T	F	M	T	W	T	F							
																									1						
																									2						
																									3						
																									4						
																									5						
																									6						
																									7						
																									8						
																									9						
																									10						
																									11						
																									12						
																									13						
																									14						
																									15						
																									16						
																									17						
																									18						
																									19						
																									20						
																									21						
																									22						
																									23						
																									24						
																									25						
																									26						
																									27						
																									28						
																									29						
																									30						
																									31						
																									32						
																									33						
																									34						
																									35						
																									36						

Subject ____________________

Week	Week___					Week___					Week___					Week___					Week___				
Day	M	T	W	T	F	M	T	W	T	F	M	T	W	T	F	M	T	W	T	F	M	T	W	T	F
Date																									
Assignments or Attendance																									
Name																									
1																									
2																									
3																									
4																									
5																									
6																									
7																									
8																									
9																									
10																									
11																									
12																									
13																									
14																									
15																									
16																									
17																									
18																									
19																									
20																									
21																									
22																									
23																									
24																									
25																									
26																									
27																									
28																									
29																									
30																									
31																									
32																									
33																									
34																									
35																									
36																									

Period ____________________

Week____					Week____					Week____					Week____					Week____						Days Present	Days Absent	Tardies	Quarter Grade		
M	T	W	T	F	M	T	W	T	F	M	T	W	T	F	M	T	W	T	F	M	T	W	T	F							
																									1						
																									2						
																									3						
																									4						
																									5						
																									6						
																									7						
																									8						
																									9						
																									10						
																									11						
																									12						
																									13						
																									14						
																									15						
																									16						
																									17						
																									18						
																									19						
																									20						
																									21						
																									22						
																									23						
																									24						
																									25						
																									26						
																									27						
																									28						
																									29						
																									30						
																									31						
																									32						
																									33						
																									34						
																									35						
																									36						

Subject ____________________

Week	Week____					Week____					Week____					Week____					Week____				
Day	M	T	W	T	F	M	T	W	T	F	M	T	W	T	F	M	T	W	T	F	M	T	W	T	F
Date																									
Assignments or Attendance																									
Name																									
1																									
2																									
3																									
4																									
5																									
6																									
7																									
8																									
9																									
10																									
11																									
12																									
13																									
14																									
15																									
16																									
17																									
18																									
19																									
20																									
21																									
22																									
23																									
24																									
25																									
26																									
27																									
28																									
29																									
30																									
31																									
32																									
33																									
34																									
35																									
36																									

Period ____________________

Week____					Week____					Week____					Week____					Week____						Days Present	Days Absent	Tardies	Quarter Grade		
M	T	W	T	F	M	T	W	T	F	M	T	W	T	F	M	T	W	T	F	M	T	W	T	F							
																									1						
																									2						
																									3						
																									4						
																									5						
																									6						
																									7						
																									8						
																									9						
																									10						
																									11						
																									12						
																									13						
																									14						
																									15						
																									16						
																									17						
																									18						
																									19						
																									20						
																									21						
																									22						
																									23						
																									24						
																									25						
																									26						
																									27						
																									28						
																									29						
																									30						
																									31						
																									32						
																									33						
																									34						
																									35						
																									36						

Subject ______________________________

Week	Week ____					Week ____					Week ____					Week ____					Week ____				
Day	M	T	W	T	F	M	T	W	T	F	M	T	W	T	F	M	T	W	T	F	M	T	W	T	F
Date																									
Assignments or Attendance																									
Name																									
1																									
2																									
3																									
4																									
5																									
6																									
7																									
8																									
9																									
10																									
11																									
12																									
13																									
14																									
15																									
16																									
17																									
18																									
19																									
20																									
21																									
22																									
23																									
24																									
25																									
26																									
27																									
28																									
29																									
30																									
31																									
32																									
33																									
34																									
35																									
36																									

Period ____________________

Week____					Week____					Week____					Week____					Week____											
M	T	W	T	F	M	T	W	T	F	M	T	W	T	F	M	T	W	T	F	M	T	W	T	F		Days Present	Days Absent	Tardies	Quarter Grade		
																									1						
																									2						
																									3						
																									4						
																									5						
																									6						
																									7						
																									8						
																									9						
																									10						
																									11						
																									12						
																									13						
																									14						
																									15						
																									16						
																									17						
																									18						
																									19						
																									20						
																									21						
																									22						
																									23						
																									24						
																									25						
																									26						
																									27						
																									28						
																									29						
																									30						
																									31						
																									32						
																									33						
																									34						
																									35						
																									36						

Subject ____________________

Week	Week ____					Week ____					Week ____					Week ____					Week ____				
Day	M	T	W	T	F	M	T	W	T	F	M	T	W	T	F	M	T	W	T	F	M	T	W	T	F
Date																									
Assignments or Attendance																									
Name																									
1																									
2																									
3																									
4																									
5																									
6																									
7																									
8																									
9																									
10																									
11																									
12																									
13																									
14																									
15																									
16																									
17																									
18																									
19																									
20																									
21																									
22																									
23																									
24																									
25																									
26																									
27																									
28																									
29																									
30																									
31																									
32																									
33																									
34																									
35																									
36																									

Period ____________________

Week____					Week____					Week____					Week____					Week____						Days Present	Days Absent	Tardies	Quarter Grade		
M	T	W	T	F	M	T	W	T	F	M	T	W	T	F	M	T	W	T	F	M	T	W	T	F							
																									1						
																									2						
																									3						
																									4						
																									5						
																									6						
																									7						
																									8						
																									9						
																									10						
																									11						
																									12						
																									13						
																									14						
																									15						
																									16						
																									17						
																									18						
																									19						
																									20						
																									21						
																									22						
																									23						
																									24						
																									25						
																									26						
																									27						
																									28						
																									29						
																									30						
																									31						
																									32						
																									33						
																									34						
																									35						
																									36						

Subject ____________________

Week	Week ___					Week ___					Week ___					Week ___					Week ___				
Day	M	T	W	T	F	M	T	W	T	F	M	T	W	T	F	M	T	W	T	F	M	T	W	T	F
Date																									
Assignments or Attendance																									
Name																									
1																									
2																									
3																									
4																									
5																									
6																									
7																									
8																									
9																									
10																									
11																									
12																									
13																									
14																									
15																									
16																									
17																									
18																									
19																									
20																									
21																									
22																									
23																									
24																									
25																									
26																									
27																									
28																									
29																									
30																									
31																									
32																									
33																									
34																									
35																									
36																									

Period ____________________

Week____					Week____					Week____					Week____					Week____						Days Present	Days Absent	Tardies	Quarter Grade		
M	T	W	T	F	M	T	W	T	F	M	T	W	T	F	M	T	W	T	F	M	T	W	T	F							
																									1						
																									2						
																									3						
																									4						
																									5						
																									6						
																									7						
																									8						
																									9						
																									10						
																									11						
																									12						
																									13						
																									14						
																									15						
																									16						
																									17						
																									18						
																									19						
																									20						
																									21						
																									22						
																									23						
																									24						
																									25						
																									26						
																									27						
																									28						
																									29						
																									30						
																									31						
																									32						
																									33						
																									34						
																									35						
																									36						

Subject ______________________

Week	Week ____					Week ____					Week ____					Week ____					Week ____				
Day	M	T	W	T	F	M	T	W	T	F	M	T	W	T	F	M	T	W	T	F	M	T	W	T	F
Date																									
Assignments or Attendance																									
Name																									
1																									
2																									
3																									
4																									
5																									
6																									
7																									
8																									
9																									
10																									
11																									
12																									
13																									
14																									
15																									
16																									
17																									
18																									
19																									
20																									
21																									
22																									
23																									
24																									
25																									
26																									
27																									
28																									
29																									
30																									
31																									
32																									
33																									
34																									
35																									
36																									

Period ____________________

Week____					Week____					Week____					Week____					Week____						Days Present	Days Absent	Tardies	Quarter Grade		
M	T	W	T	F	M	T	W	T	F	M	T	W	T	F	M	T	W	T	F	M	T	W	T	F							
																									1						
																									2						
																									3						
																									4						
																									5						
																									6						
																									7						
																									8						
																									9						
																									10						
																									11						
																									12						
																									13						
																									14						
																									15						
																									16						
																									17						
																									18						
																									19						
																									20						
																									21						
																									22						
																									23						
																									24						
																									25						
																									26						
																									27						
																									28						
																									29						
																									30						
																									31						
																									32						
																									33						
																									34						
																									35						
																									36						

Subject ____________________

Week	Week ____					Week ____					Week ____					Week ____					Week ____				
Day	M	T	W	T	F	M	T	W	T	F	M	T	W	T	F	M	T	W	T	F	M	T	W	T	F
Date																									
Assignments or Attendance																									
Name																									
1																									
2																									
3																									
4																									
5																									
6																									
7																									
8																									
9																									
10																									
11																									
12																									
13																									
14																									
15																									
16																									
17																									
18																									
19																									
20																									
21																									
22																									
23																									
24																									
25																									
26																									
27																									
28																									
29																									
30																									
31																									
32																									
33																									
34																									
35																									
36																									

Period ____________________

Week____					Week____					Week____					Week____					Week____						Days Present	Days Absent	Tardies	Quarter Grade		
M	T	W	T	F	M	T	W	T	F	M	T	W	T	F	M	T	W	T	F	M	T	W	T	F							
																									1						
																									2						
																									3						
																									4						
																									5						
																									6						
																									7						
																									8						
																									9						
																									10						
																									11						
																									12						
																									13						
																									14						
																									15						
																									16						
																									17						
																									18						
																									19						
																									20						
																									21						
																									22						
																									23						
																									24						
																									25						
																									26						
																									27						
																									28						
																									29						
																									30						
																									31						
																									32						
																									33						
																									34						
																									35						
																									36						

Subject________________________

Week	Week____					Week____					Week____					Week____					Week____				
Day	M	T	W	T	F	M	T	W	T	F	M	T	W	T	F	M	T	W	T	F	M	T	W	T	F
Date																									
Assignments or Attendance																									
Name																									
1																									
2																									
3																									
4																									
5																									
6																									
7																									
8																									
9																									
10																									
11																									
12																									
13																									
14																									
15																									
16																									
17																									
18																									
19																									
20																									
21																									
22																									
23																									
24																									
25																									
26																									
27																									
28																									
29																									
30																									
31																									
32																									
33																									
34																									
35																									
36																									

Period____________________

Week____					Week____					Week____					Week____					Week____						Days Present	Days Absent	Tardies	Quarter Grade		
M	T	W	T	F	M	T	W	T	F	M	T	W	T	F	M	T	W	T	F	M	T	W	T	F							
																									1						
																									2						
																									3						
																									4						
																									5						
																									6						
																									7						
																									8						
																									9						
																									10						
																									11						
																									12						
																									13						
																									14						
																									15						
																									16						
																									17						
																									18						
																									19						
																									20						
																									21						
																									22						
																									23						
																									24						
																									25						
																									26						
																									27						
																									28						
																									29						
																									30						
																									31						
																									32						
																									33						
																									34						
																									35						
																									36						

Subject ______________________

Week	Week ____					Week ____					Week ____					Week ____					Week ____				
Day	M	T	W	T	F	M	T	W	T	F	M	T	W	T	F	M	T	W	T	F	M	T	W	T	F
Date																									
Assignments or Attendance																									
Name																									
1																									
2																									
3																									
4																									
5																									
6																									
7																									
8																									
9																									
10																									
11																									
12																									
13																									
14																									
15																									
16																									
17																									
18																									
19																									
20																									
21																									
22																									
23																									
24																									
25																									
26																									
27																									
28																									
29																									
30																									
31																									
32																									
33																									
34																									
35																									
36																									

Period ____________________

Week ____					Week ____					Week ____					Week ____					Week ____						Days Present	Days Absent	Tardies	Quarter Grade		
M	T	W	T	F	M	T	W	T	F	M	T	W	T	F	M	T	W	T	F	M	T	W	T	F							
																									1						
																									2						
																									3						
																									4						
																									5						
																									6						
																									7						
																									8						
																									9						
																									10						
																									11						
																									12						
																									13						
																									14						
																									15						
																									16						
																									17						
																									18						
																									19						
																									20						
																									21						
																									22						
																									23						
																									24						
																									25						
																									26						
																									27						
																									28						
																									29						
																									30						
																									31						
																									32						
																									33						
																									34						
																									35						
																									36						

Subject____________________

Week	Week____					Week____					Week____					Week____					Week____				
Day	M	T	W	T	F	M	T	W	T	F	M	T	W	T	F	M	T	W	T	F	M	T	W	T	F
Date																									
Assignments or Attendance																									
Name																									
1																									
2																									
3																									
4																									
5																									
6																									
7																									
8																									
9																									
10																									
11																									
12																									
13																									
14																									
15																									
16																									
17																									
18																									
19																									
20																									
21																									
22																									
23																									
24																									
25																									
26																									
27																									
28																									
29																									
30																									
31																									
32																									
33																									
34																									
35																									
36																									

Period ____________________

Week____					Week____					Week____					Week____					Week____						Days Present	Days Absent	Tardies	Quarter Grade		
M	T	W	T	F	M	T	W	T	F	M	T	W	T	F	M	T	W	T	F	M	T	W	T	F							
																									1						
																									2						
																									3						
																									4						
																									5						
																									6						
																									7						
																									8						
																									9						
																									10						
																									11						
																									12						
																									13						
																									14						
																									15						
																									16						
																									17						
																									18						
																									19						
																									20						
																									21						
																									22						
																									23						
																									24						
																									25						
																									26						
																									27						
																									28						
																									29						
																									30						
																									31						
																									32						
																									33						
																									34						
																									35						
																									36						

Subject ____________________

Week	Week ____					Week ____					Week ____					Week ____					Week ____				
Day	M	T	W	T	F	M	T	W	T	F	M	T	W	T	F	M	T	W	T	F	M	T	W	T	F
Date																									
Assignments or Attendance																									
Name																									
1																									
2																									
3																									
4																									
5																									
6																									
7																									
8																									
9																									
10																									
11																									
12																									
13																									
14																									
15																									
16																									
17																									
18																									
19																									
20																									
21																									
22																									
23																									
24																									
25																									
26																									
27																									
28																									
29																									
30																									
31																									
32																									
33																									
34																									
35																									
36																									

Period ____________________

Week____					Week____					Week____					Week____					Week____						Days Present	Days Absent	Tardies	Quarter Grade		
M	T	W	T	F	M	T	W	T	F	M	T	W	T	F	M	T	W	T	F	M	T	W	T	F							
																									1						
																									2						
																									3						
																									4						
																									5						
																									6						
																									7						
																									8						
																									9						
																									10						
																									11						
																									12						
																									13						
																									14						
																									15						
																									16						
																									17						
																									18						
																									19						
																									20						
																									21						
																									22						
																									23						
																									24						
																									25						
																									26						
																									27						
																									28						
																									29						
																									30						
																									31						
																									32						
																									33						
																									34						
																									35						
																									36						

Subject_______________

Week	Week____					Week____					Week____					Week____					Week____				
Day	M	T	W	T	F	M	T	W	T	F	M	T	W	T	F	M	T	W	T	F	M	T	W	T	F
Date																									
Assignments or Attendance																									
Name																									
1																									
2																									
3																									
4																									
5																									
6																									
7																									
8																									
9																									
10																									
11																									
12																									
13																									
14																									
15																									
16																									
17																									
18																									
19																									
20																									
21																									
22																									
23																									
24																									
25																									
26																									
27																									
28																									
29																									
30																									
31																									
32																									
33																									
34																									
35																									
36																									

Period ____________________

Week____					Week____					Week____					Week____					Week____						Days Present	Days Absent	Tardies	Quarter Grade		
M	T	W	T	F	M	T	W	T	F	M	T	W	T	F	M	T	W	T	F	M	T	W	T	F							
																									1						
																									2						
																									3						
																									4						
																									5						
																									6						
																									7						
																									8						
																									9						
																									10						
																									11						
																									12						
																									13						
																									14						
																									15						
																									16						
																									17						
																									18						
																									19						
																									20						
																									21						
																									22						
																									23						
																									24						
																									25						
																									26						
																									27						
																									28						
																									29						
																									30						
																									31						
																									32						
																									33						
																									34						
																									35						
																									36						

Subject ____________________

Week	Week____					Week____					Week____					Week____					Week____				
Day	M	T	W	T	F	M	T	W	T	F	M	T	W	T	F	M	T	W	T	F	M	T	W	T	F
Date																									
Assignments or Attendance																									
Name																									
1																									
2																									
3																									
4																									
5																									
6																									
7																									
8																									
9																									
10																									
11																									
12																									
13																									
14																									
15																									
16																									
17																									
18																									
19																									
20																									
21																									
22																									
23																									
24																									
25																									
26																									
27																									
28																									
29																									
30																									
31																									
32																									
33																									
34																									
35																									
36																									

Period ____________________

Week____					Week____					Week____					Week____					Week____						Days Present	Days Absent	Tardies	Quarter Grade		
M	T	W	T	F	M	T	W	T	F	M	T	W	T	F	M	T	W	T	F	M	T	W	T	F							
																									1						
																									2						
																									3						
																									4						
																									5						
																									6						
																									7						
																									8						
																									9						
																									10						
																									11						
																									12						
																									13						
																									14						
																									15						
																									16						
																									17						
																									18						
																									19						
																									20						
																									21						
																									22						
																									23						
																									24						
																									25						
																									26						
																									27						
																									28						
																									29						
																									30						
																									31						
																									32						
																									33						
																									34						
																									35						
																									36						

Subject ____________________

Week	Week____					Week____					Week____					Week____					Week____				
Day	M	T	W	T	F	M	T	W	T	F	M	T	W	T	F	M	T	W	T	F	M	T	W	T	F
Date																									
Assignments or Attendance																									
Name																									
1																									
2																									
3																									
4																									
5																									
6																									
7																									
8																									
9																									
10																									
11																									
12																									
13																									
14																									
15																									
16																									
17																									
18																									
19																									
20																									
21																									
22																									
23																									
24																									
25																									
26																									
27																									
28																									
29																									
30																									
31																									
32																									
33																									
34																									
35																									
36																									

Period ______________________

Week____					Week____					Week____					Week____					Week____						Days Present	Days Absent	Tardies	Quarter Grade		
M	T	W	T	F	M	T	W	T	F	M	T	W	T	F	M	T	W	T	F	M	T	W	T	F							
																									1						
																									2						
																									3						
																									4						
																									5						
																									6						
																									7						
																									8						
																									9						
																									10						
																									11						
																									12						
																									13						
																									14						
																									15						
																									16						
																									17						
																									18						
																									19						
																									20						
																									21						
																									22						
																									23						
																									24						
																									25						
																									26						
																									27						
																									28						
																									29						
																									30						
																									31						
																									32						
																									33						
																									34						
																									35						
																									36						

Subject ______________________

Week	Week ____					Week ____					Week ____					Week ____					Week ____				
Day	M	T	W	T	F	M	T	W	T	F	M	T	W	T	F	M	T	W	T	F	M	T	W	T	F
Date																									
Assignments or Attendance																									
Name																									
1																									
2																									
3																									
4																									
5																									
6																									
7																									
8																									
9																									
10																									
11																									
12																									
13																									
14																									
15																									
16																									
17																									
18																									
19																									
20																									
21																									
22																									
23																									
24																									
25																									
26																									
27																									
28																									
29																									
30																									
31																									
32																									
33																									
34																									
35																									
36																									

Period ____________________________

Week ___					Week ___					Week ___					Week ___					Week ___						Days Present	Days Absent	Tardies	Quarter Grade		
M	T	W	T	F	M	T	W	T	F	M	T	W	T	F	M	T	W	T	F	M	T	W	T	F							
																									1						
																									2						
																									3						
																									4						
																									5						
																									6						
																									7						
																									8						
																									9						
																									10						
																									11						
																									12						
																									13						
																									14						
																									15						
																									16						
																									17						
																									18						
																									19						
																									20						
																									21						
																									22						
																									23						
																									24						
																									25						
																									26						
																									27						
																									28						
																									29						
																									30						
																									31						
																									32						
																									33						
																									34						
																									35						
																									36						

Subject ____________________

Week	Week ____					Week ____					Week ____					Week ____					Week ____				
Day	M	T	W	T	F	M	T	W	T	F	M	T	W	T	F	M	T	W	T	F	M	T	W	T	F
Date																									
Assignments or Attendance																									
Name																									
1																									
2																									
3																									
4																									
5																									
6																									
7																									
8																									
9																									
10																									
11																									
12																									
13																									
14																									
15																									
16																									
17																									
18																									
19																									
20																									
21																									
22																									
23																									
24																									
25																									
26																									
27																									
28																									
29																									
30																									
31																									
32																									
33																									
34																									
35																									
36																									

Period ____________________

Week____					Week____					Week____					Week____					Week____						Days Present	Days Absent	Tardies	Quarter Grade		
M	T	W	T	F	M	T	W	T	F	M	T	W	T	F	M	T	W	T	F	M	T	W	T	F							
																									1						
																									2						
																									3						
																									4						
																									5						
																									6						
																									7						
																									8						
																									9						
																									10						
																									11						
																									12						
																									13						
																									14						
																									15						
																									16						
																									17						
																									18						
																									19						
																									20						
																									21						
																									22						
																									23						
																									24						
																									25						
																									26						
																									27						
																									28						
																									29						
																									30						
																									31						
																									32						
																									33						
																									34						
																									35						
																									36						

Subject ____________________

Week	Week ___					Week ___					Week ___					Week ___					Week ___				
Day	M	T	W	T	F	M	T	W	T	F	M	T	W	T	F	M	T	W	T	F	M	T	W	T	F
Date																									
Assignments or Attendance																									
Name																									
1																									
2																									
3																									
4																									
5																									
6																									
7																									
8																									
9																									
10																									
11																									
12																									
13																									
14																									
15																									
16																									
17																									
18																									
19																									
20																									
21																									
22																									
23																									
24																									
25																									
26																									
27																									
28																									
29																									
30																									
31																									
32																									
33																									
34																									
35																									
36																									

Period ____________________

Week____					Week____					Week____					Week____					Week____						Days Present	Days Absent	Tardies	Quarter Grade		
M	T	W	T	F	M	T	W	T	F	M	T	W	T	F	M	T	W	T	F	M	T	W	T	F							
																									1						
																									2						
																									3						
																									4						
																									5						
																									6						
																									7						
																									8						
																									9						
																									10						
																									11						
																									12						
																									13						
																									14						
																									15						
																									16						
																									17						
																									18						
																									19						
																									20						
																									21						
																									22						
																									23						
																									24						
																									25						
																									26						
																									27						
																									28						
																									29						
																									30						
																									31						
																									32						
																									33						
																									34						
																									35						
																									36						

Subject ____________________

Week	Week ____					Week ____					Week ____					Week ____					Week ____				
Day	M	T	W	T	F	M	T	W	T	F	M	T	W	T	F	M	T	W	T	F	M	T	W	T	F
Date																									
Assignments or Attendance																									
Name																									
1																									
2																									
3																									
4																									
5																									
6																									
7																									
8																									
9																									
10																									
11																									
12																									
13																									
14																									
15																									
16																									
17																									
18																									
19																									
20																									
21																									
22																									
23																									
24																									
25																									
26																									
27																									
28																									
29																									
30																									
31																									
32																									
33																									
34																									
35																									
36																									

Period ____________________

Week____					Week____					Week____					Week____					Week____						Days Present	Days Absent	Tardies	Quarter Grade		
M	T	W	T	F	M	T	W	T	F	M	T	W	T	F	M	T	W	T	F	M	T	W	T	F							
																									1						
																									2						
																									3						
																									4						
																									5						
																									6						
																									7						
																									8						
																									9						
																									10						
																									11						
																									12						
																									13						
																									14						
																									15						
																									16						
																									17						
																									18						
																									19						
																									20						
																									21						
																									22						
																									23						
																									24						
																									25						
																									26						
																									27						
																									28						
																									29						
																									30						
																									31						
																									32						
																									33						
																									34						
																									35						
																									36						

Subject ______________________________

Week	Week____					Week____					Week____					Week____					Week____				
Day	M	T	W	T	F	M	T	W	T	F	M	T	W	T	F	M	T	W	T	F	M	T	W	T	F
Date																									
Assignments or Attendance																									
Name																									
1																									
2																									
3																									
4																									
5																									
6																									
7																									
8																									
9																									
10																									
11																									
12																									
13																									
14																									
15																									
16																									
17																									
18																									
19																									
20																									
21																									
22																									
23																									
24																									
25																									
26																									
27																									
28																									
29																									
30																									
31																									
32																									
33																									
34																									
35																									
36																									

Period ____________________

Week____					Week____					Week____					Week____					Week____						Days Present	Days Absent	Tardies	Quarter Grade		
M	T	W	T	F	M	T	W	T	F	M	T	W	T	F	M	T	W	T	F	M	T	W	T	F							
																									1						
																									2						
																									3						
																									4						
																									5						
																									6						
																									7						
																									8						
																									9						
																									10						
																									11						
																									12						
																									13						
																									14						
																									15						
																									16						
																									17						
																									18						
																									19						
																									20						
																									21						
																									22						
																									23						
																									24						
																									25						
																									26						
																									27						
																									28						
																									29						
																									30						
																									31						
																									32						
																									33						
																									34						
																									35						
																									36						

Subject ____________

Week	Week____					Week____					Week____					Week____					Week____				
Day	M	T	W	T	F	M	T	W	T	F	M	T	W	T	F	M	T	W	T	F	M	T	W	T	F
Date																									
Assignments or Attendance																									
Name																									
1																									
2																									
3																									
4																									
5																									
6																									
7																									
8																									
9																									
10																									
11																									
12																									
13																									
14																									
15																									
16																									
17																									
18																									
19																									
20																									
21																									
22																									
23																									
24																									
25																									
26																									
27																									
28																									
29																									
30																									
31																									
32																									
33																									
34																									
35																									
36																									

Period ____________________

Week____					Week____					Week____					Week____					Week____						Days Present	Days Absent	Tardies	Quarter Grade		
M	T	W	T	F	M	T	W	T	F	M	T	W	T	F	M	T	W	T	F	M	T	W	T	F							
																									1						
																									2						
																									3						
																									4						
																									5						
																									6						
																									7						
																									8						
																									9						
																									10						
																									11						
																									12						
																									13						
																									14						
																									15						
																									16						
																									17						
																									18						
																									19						
																									20						
																									21						
																									22						
																									23						
																									24						
																									25						
																									26						
																									27						
																									28						
																									29						
																									30						
																									31						
																									32						
																									33						
																									34						
																									35						
																									36						

Subject ______________________

Week	Week____					Week____					Week____					Week____					Week____				
Day	M	T	W	T	F	M	T	W	T	F	M	T	W	T	F	M	T	W	T	F	M	T	W	T	F
Date																									
Assignments or Attendance																									
Name																									
1																									
2																									
3																									
4																									
5																									
6																									
7																									
8																									
9																									
10																									
11																									
12																									
13																									
14																									
15																									
16																									
17																									
18																									
19																									
20																									
21																									
22																									
23																									
24																									
25																									
26																									
27																									
28																									
29																									
30																									
31																									
32																									
33																									
34																									
35																									
36																									

Period ____________________

Week____					Week____					Week____					Week____					Week____						Days Present	Days Absent	Tardies	Quarter Grade		
M	T	W	T	F	M	T	W	T	F	M	T	W	T	F	M	T	W	T	F	M	T	W	T	F							
																									1						
																									2						
																									3						
																									4						
																									5						
																									6						
																									7						
																									8						
																									9						
																									10						
																									11						
																									12						
																									13						
																									14						
																									15						
																									16						
																									17						
																									18						
																									19						
																									20						
																									21						
																									22						
																									23						
																									24						
																									25						
																									26						
																									27						
																									28						
																									29						
																									30						
																									31						
																									32						
																									33						
																									34						
																									35						
																									36						

Subject ________________________

Week	Week____					Week____					Week____					Week____					Week____				
Day	M	T	W	T	F	M	T	W	T	F	M	T	W	T	F	M	T	W	T	F	M	T	W	T	F
Date																									
Assignments or Attendance																									
Name																									
1																									
2																									
3																									
4																									
5																									
6																									
7																									
8																									
9																									
10																									
11																									
12																									
13																									
14																									
15																									
16																									
17																									
18																									
19																									
20																									
21																									
22																									
23																									
24																									
25																									
26																									
27																									
28																									
29																									
30																									
31																									
32																									
33																									
34																									
35																									
36																									

Period ________________________________

Week____					Week____					Week____					Week____					Week____						Days Present	Days Absent	Tardies	Quarter Grade		
M	T	W	T	F	M	T	W	T	F	M	T	W	T	F	M	T	W	T	F	M	T	W	T	F							
																									1						
																									2						
																									3						
																									4						
																									5						
																									6						
																									7						
																									8						
																									9						
																									10						
																									11						
																									12						
																									13						
																									14						
																									15						
																									16						
																									17						
																									18						
																									19						
																									20						
																									21						
																									22						
																									23						
																									24						
																									25						
																									26						
																									27						
																									28						
																									29						
																									30						
																									31						
																									32						
																									33						
																									34						
																									35						
																									36						

Subject ________________

Week	Week ____					Week ____					Week ____					Week ____					Week ____				
Day	M	T	W	T	F	M	T	W	T	F	M	T	W	T	F	M	T	W	T	F	M	T	W	T	F
Date																									
Assignments or Attendance																									
Name																									
1																									
2																									
3																									
4																									
5																									
6																									
7																									
8																									
9																									
10																									
11																									
12																									
13																									
14																									
15																									
16																									
17																									
18																									
19																									
20																									
21																									
22																									
23																									
24																									
25																									
26																									
27																									
28																									
29																									
30																									
31																									
32																									
33																									
34																									
35																									
36																									

Period ______________________________

Week____					Week____					Week____					Week____					Week____						Days Present	Days Absent	Tardies	Quarter Grade		
M	T	W	T	F	M	T	W	T	F	M	T	W	T	F	M	T	W	T	F	M	T	W	T	F							
																									1						
																									2						
																									3						
																									4						
																									5						
																									6						
																									7						
																									8						
																									9						
																									10						
																									11						
																									12						
																									13						
																									14						
																									15						
																									16						
																									17						
																									18						
																									19						
																									20						
																									21						
																									22						
																									23						
																									24						
																									25						
																									26						
																									27						
																									28						
																									29						
																									30						
																									31						
																									32						
																									33						
																									34						
																									35						
																									36						

Notes

Lesson Plans

Week of ____________________

Monday			
Tuesday			
Wednesday			
Thursday			
Friday			

Plan, work your plan, love your work and you will have success.

–Anonymous

Week of ____________________

Monday			
Tuesday			
Wednesday			
Thursday			
Friday			

There are no gains without pains. —*Benjamin Franklin*

Week of ______________________

Monday			
Tuesday			
Wednesday			
Thursday			
Friday			

The only limit to our realization of tomorrow be our doubts of today.

—Franklin D. Roosevelt

Week of ____________________

Monday			
Tuesday			
Wednesday			
Thursday			
Friday			

Difficult things take a long time. The impossible takes a little longer.

—Unknown

Week of ______________________

Monday			
Tuesday			
Wednesday			
Thursday			
Friday			

No one can make you feel inferior without your consent.

—Eleanor Roosevelt

Week of ______________________

Monday			
Tuesday			
Wednesday			
Thursday			
Friday	We are off		

Whether you think you can or think you can't – you are right.

–Henry Ford

Week of ______________________

Monday			
Tuesday			
Wednesday			
Thursday			
Friday			

Ambition is enthusiasm with a purpose. —Unknown

Week of ____________________

Monday			
Tuesday			
Wednesday			
Thursday			
Friday			

Courage is resistance to fear, mastery of fear – not absence of fear.

–Mark Twain

Week of ______________________

Monday			
Tuesday			
Wednesday			
Thursday			
Friday			

Love truth, but pardon error. —Voltaire

Week of ____________________

Monday			
Tuesday			
Wednesday			
Thursday			
Friday			

The harder the conflict, the more glorious the triumph.

–Thomas Paine

Week of ____________________

Monday			
Tuesday			
Wednesday			
Thursday			
Friday			

I don't think much of a man who is not wiser today than he was yesterday.

—Abraham Lincoln

Week of ____________

Monday			
Tuesday			
Wednesday			
Thursday			
Friday			

The time to repair the roof is when the sun is shining.

–John F. Kennedy

Week of ____________________

Monday			
Tuesday			
Wednesday			
Thursday			
Friday			

Genius is one percent inspiration and ninety-nine percent perspiration.
—Thomas A. Edison

Week of ____________________

Monday			
Tuesday			
Wednesday			
Thursday			
Friday			

Success is counted sweetest, by those who ne'er succeed.

—Emily Dickinson

Week of ______________________

Monday			
Tuesday			
Wednesday			
Thursday			
Friday			

In the middle of difficulty lies opportunity.

—Albert Einstein

Week of ______________________

Monday			
Tuesday			
Wednesday			
Thursday			
Friday			

The first and best victory is to conquer self. —Plato

Week of ____________________

Monday			
Tuesday			
Wednesday			
Thursday			
Friday			

No act of kindness, no matter how small, is ever wasted.

–Aesop

Week of ______________________

Monday			
Tuesday			
Wednesday			
Thursday			
Friday			

Do what you can, with what you have, where you are.

–Theodore Roosevelt

Week of ____________________

Monday			
Tuesday			
Wednesday			
Thursday			
Friday			

There's a way to do it better – find it. –Thomas A. Edison

Week of ____________________

Monday			
Tuesday			
Wednesday			
Thursday			
Friday			

Is there anyone so wise as to learn by the experience of others?

—Voltaire

Week of ______________________

Monday			
Tuesday			
Wednesday			
Thursday			
Friday			

Success is getting what you want; happiness is wanting what you get.

—Anonymous

Week of ____________________

Monday			
Tuesday 			
Wednesday 			
Thursday 			
Friday 			

We might all be successful if we followed the advice we give the other fellow.

—Anonymous

Week of ____________________

Monday			
Tuesday			
Wednesday			
Thursday			
Friday			

You can't climb the ladder of success with cold feet.

–Anonymous

Week of ______________________

Monday			
Tuesday			
Wednesday			
Thursday			
Friday			

Leadership is the ability to get men to do what they don't want to do and like doing it.

–Harry Truman

Week of ______________________

Monday			
Tuesday			
Wednesday			
Thursday			
Friday			

When you get to the end of your rope, tie a knot and hang on.

–Franklin Roosevelt

Week of ____________________

Monday			
Tuesday			
Wednesday			
Thursday			
Friday			

Actions speak louder than words, but not so often.

–Farmer's Almanac

Week of ______________________

Monday			
Tuesday			
Wednesday			
Thursday			
Friday			

If you carry with you your childhood, you never become older.

—Abraham Lincoln

Week of assesments

Monday			
Tuesday			
Wednesday			
Thursday			
Friday			

Never discourage anyone who continually makes progress, no matter how slow.

–Plato

Week of ____________________

Monday			
Tuesday			
Wednesday			
Thursday			
Friday			

Tell me and I'll forget; show me and I may remember; involve me and I'll understand.

—Chinese Proverb

Week of ________________

Monday			
Tuesday			
Wednesday			
Thursday			
Friday			

Little minds are tamed and subdued by misfortune; but great minds rise above them.
—Washington Irving

Week of ____________________

Monday			
Tuesday			
Wednesday			
Thursday			
Friday			

I must govern the clock, not be governed by it. —Golda Meir

Week of ____________________

Monday			
Tuesday			
Wednesday			
Thursday			
Friday			

A life spent making mistakes is not only more honorable but more useful than a life spent doing nothing. —George Bernard Shaw

Week of ____________________

Monday			
Tuesday			
Wednesday			
Thursday			
Friday			

Happiness is the full use of your powers along lines of excellence in a life affording scope. —John F. Kennedy

Week of ______________________

Monday			
Tuesday			
Wednesday			
Thursday			
Friday			

Hope sees the invisible, feels the intangible and achieves the impossible.

—Unknown

Week of ____________________

Monday			
Tuesday 			
Wednesday 			
Thursday			
Friday 			

Never bend your head, always hold it high. Look the world straight in the face.

–Helen Keller

Week of ____________________

Monday			
Tuesday			
Wednesday			
Thursday			
Friday			

Week of ____________________

Monday			
Tuesday			
Wednesday			
Thursday			
Friday			

A journey of a thousand miles must begin with a single step.

—Chinese Proverb

Week of ____________________

Monday			
Tuesday 			
Wednesday 			
Thursday			
Friday 			

If you aspire to the highest place, it is no disgrace to stop at the second, or even the third, place.

—Cicero

Week of ____________________

Monday			
Tuesday			
Wednesday			
Thursday			
Friday			

If better is possible, good is not enough. —Unknown

Week of ____________________

Monday			
Tuesday			
Wednesday			
Thursday			
Friday			

Some people dream of worthy accomplishments, while others stay awake and do them.

—Unknown

Week of ____________________

Monday			
Tuesday			
Wednesday			
Thursday			
Friday			

Your biggest task is not to get ahead of others, but to surpass yourself.

—Unknown

Notes

